May this coloring book be a magical world of imagination and creativity for every child who explores it. May each page be an invitation to dream, smile and express yourself with vibrant colors. May each stroke be an opportunity for discovery and learning. May the joy of coloring these pages be a reflection of the brightness and beauty that each child carries within them.

Fondly.

2024
Thainá Marques

T.M.P©
Thainá's Marques Publications

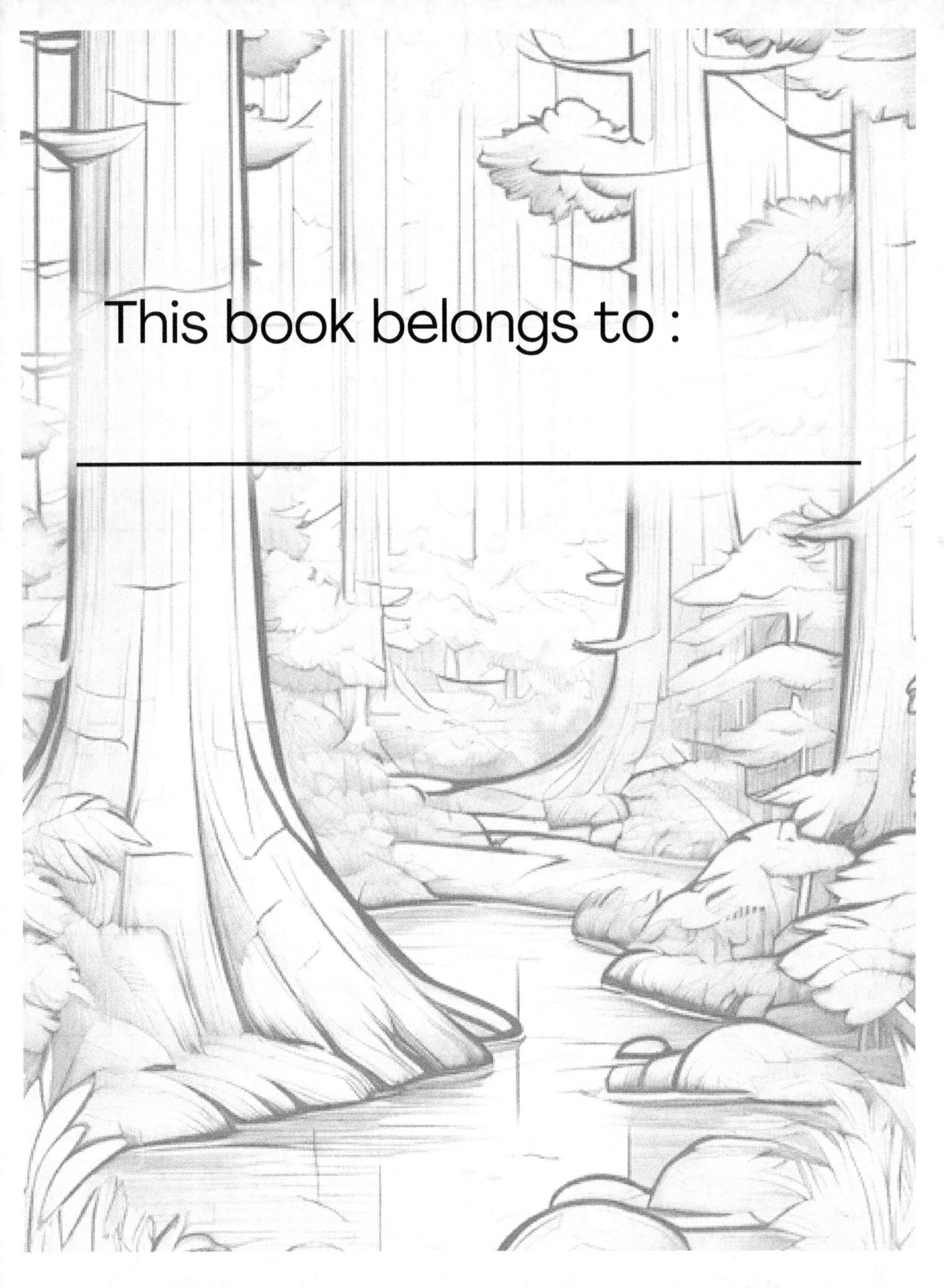

This book belongs to :

_____

Test color page

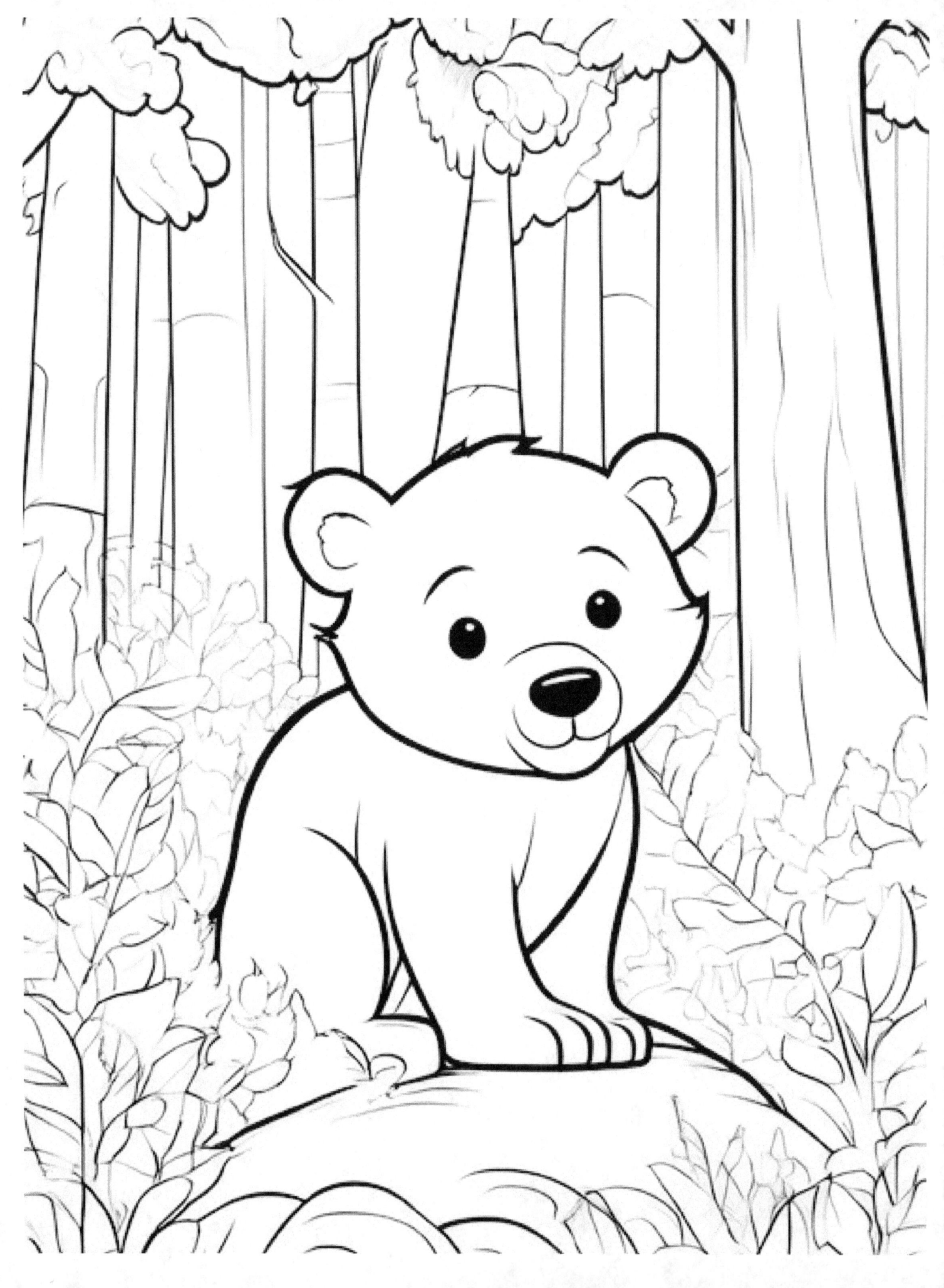

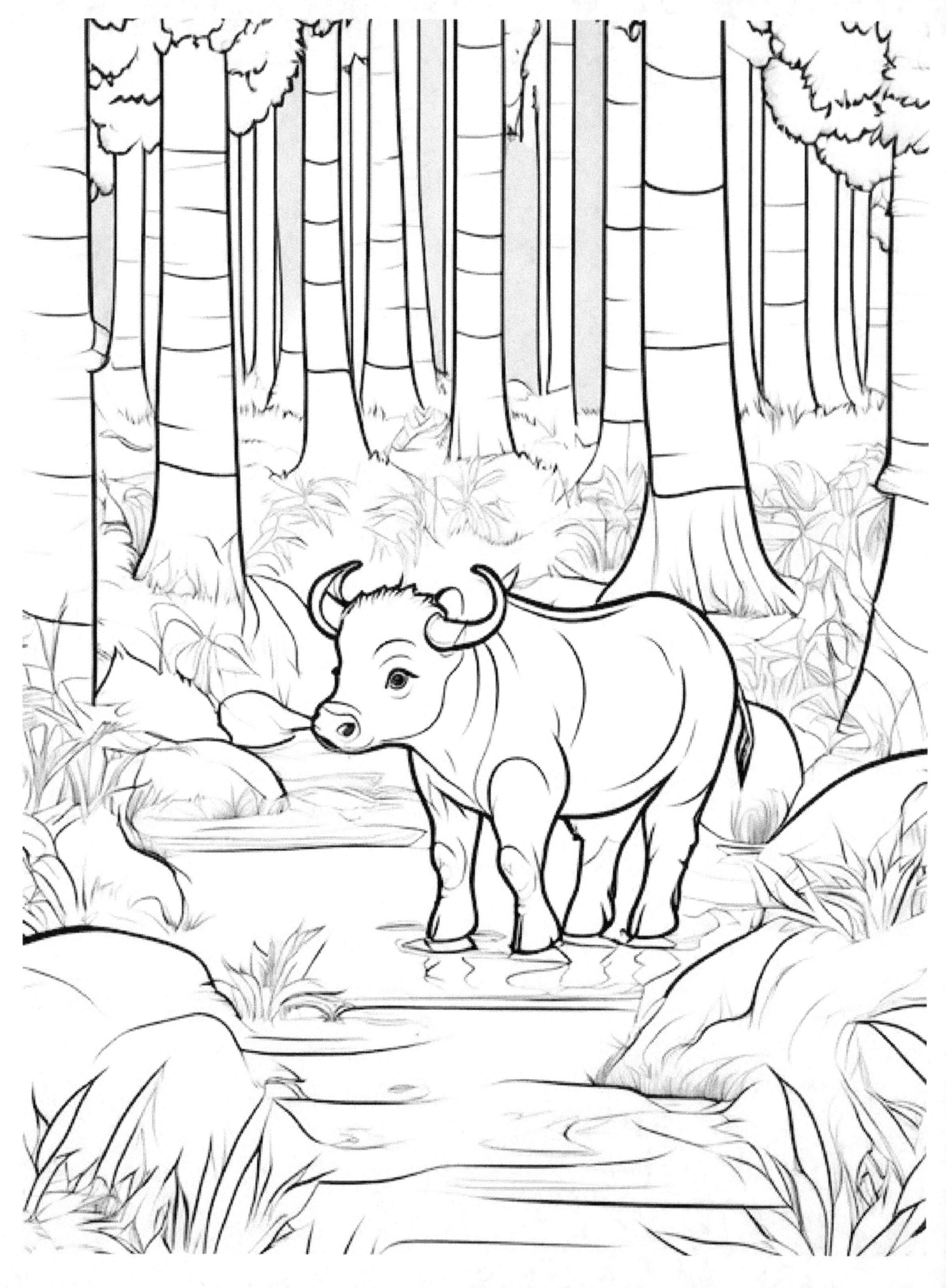

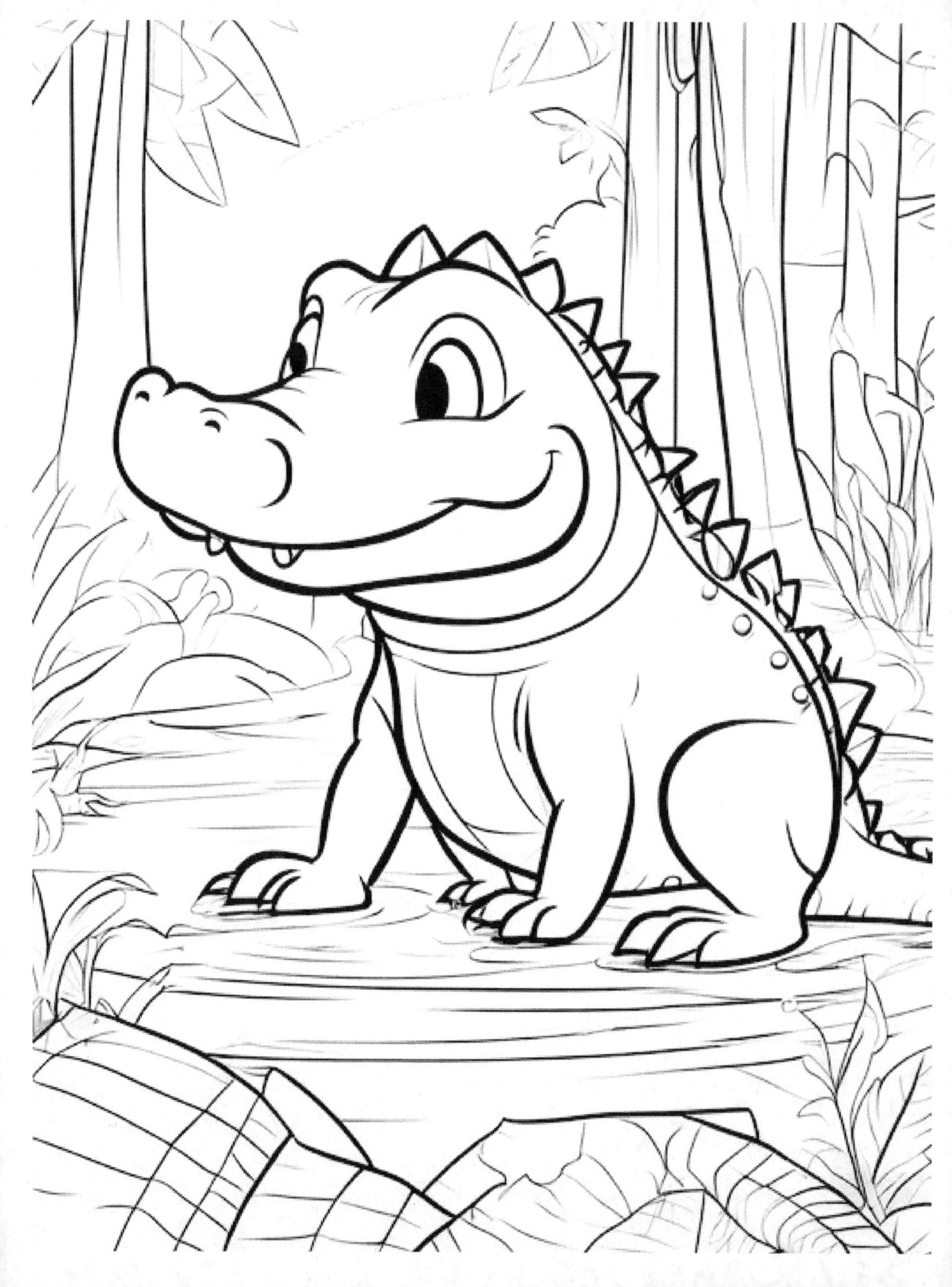

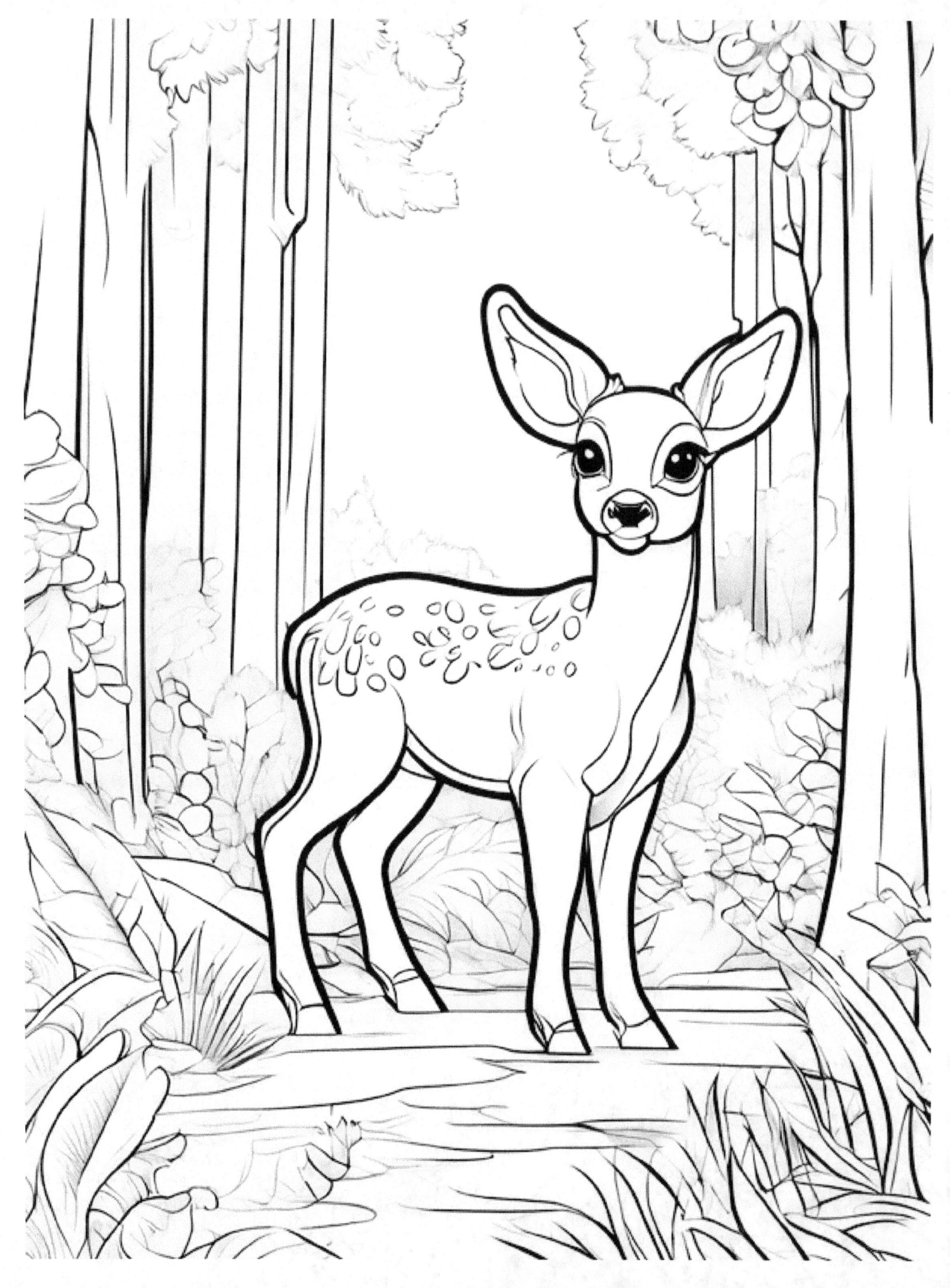

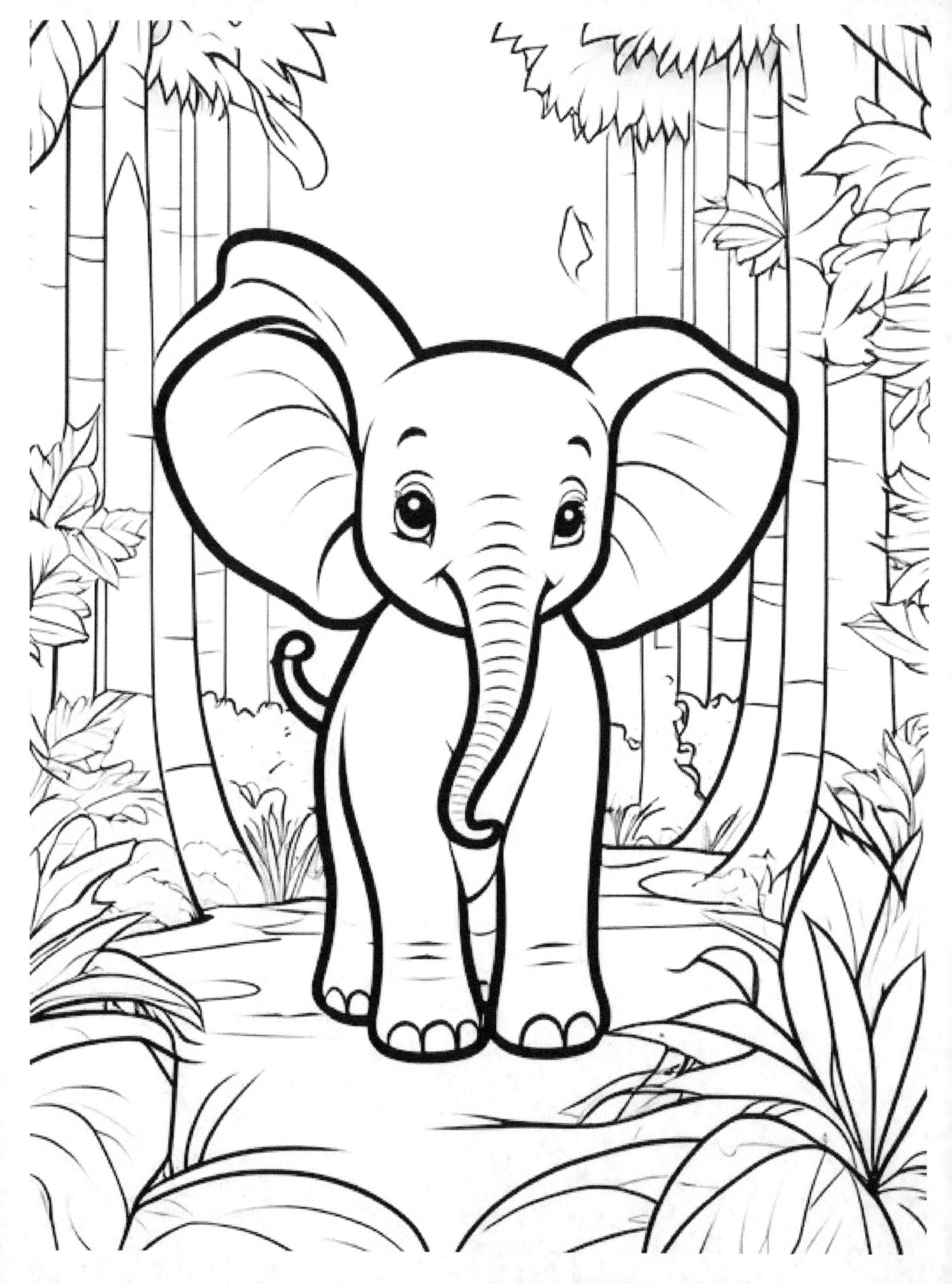

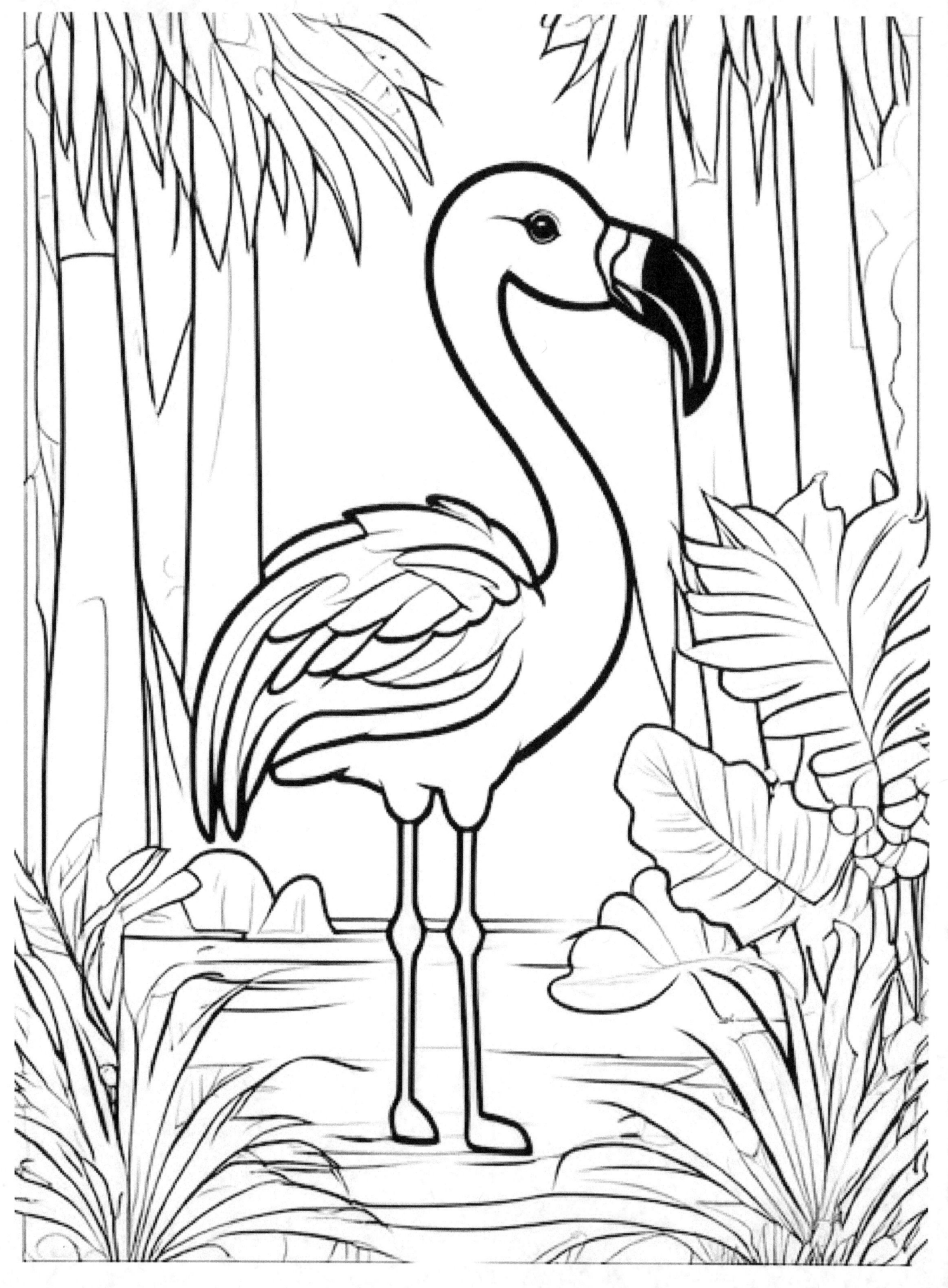

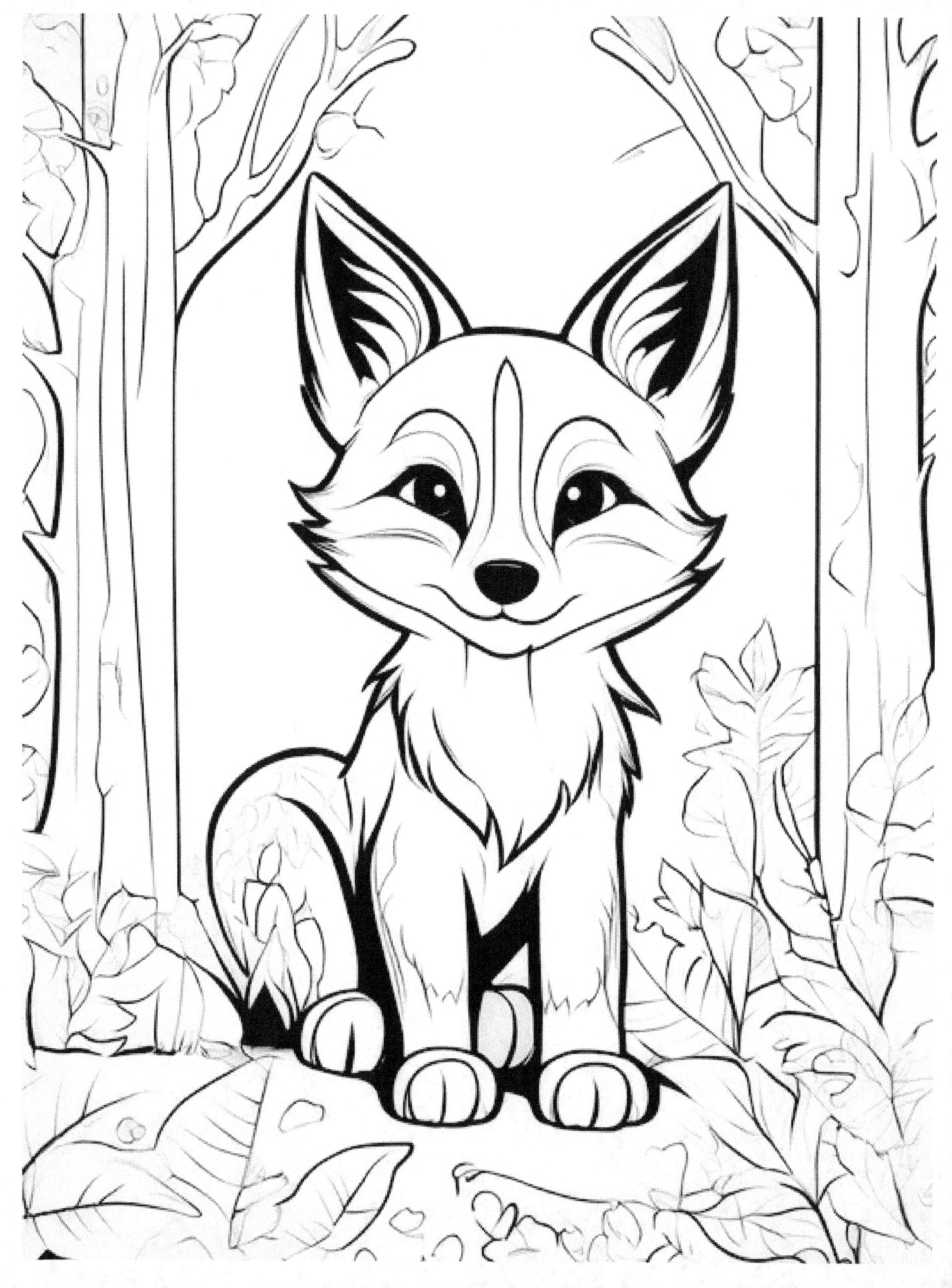

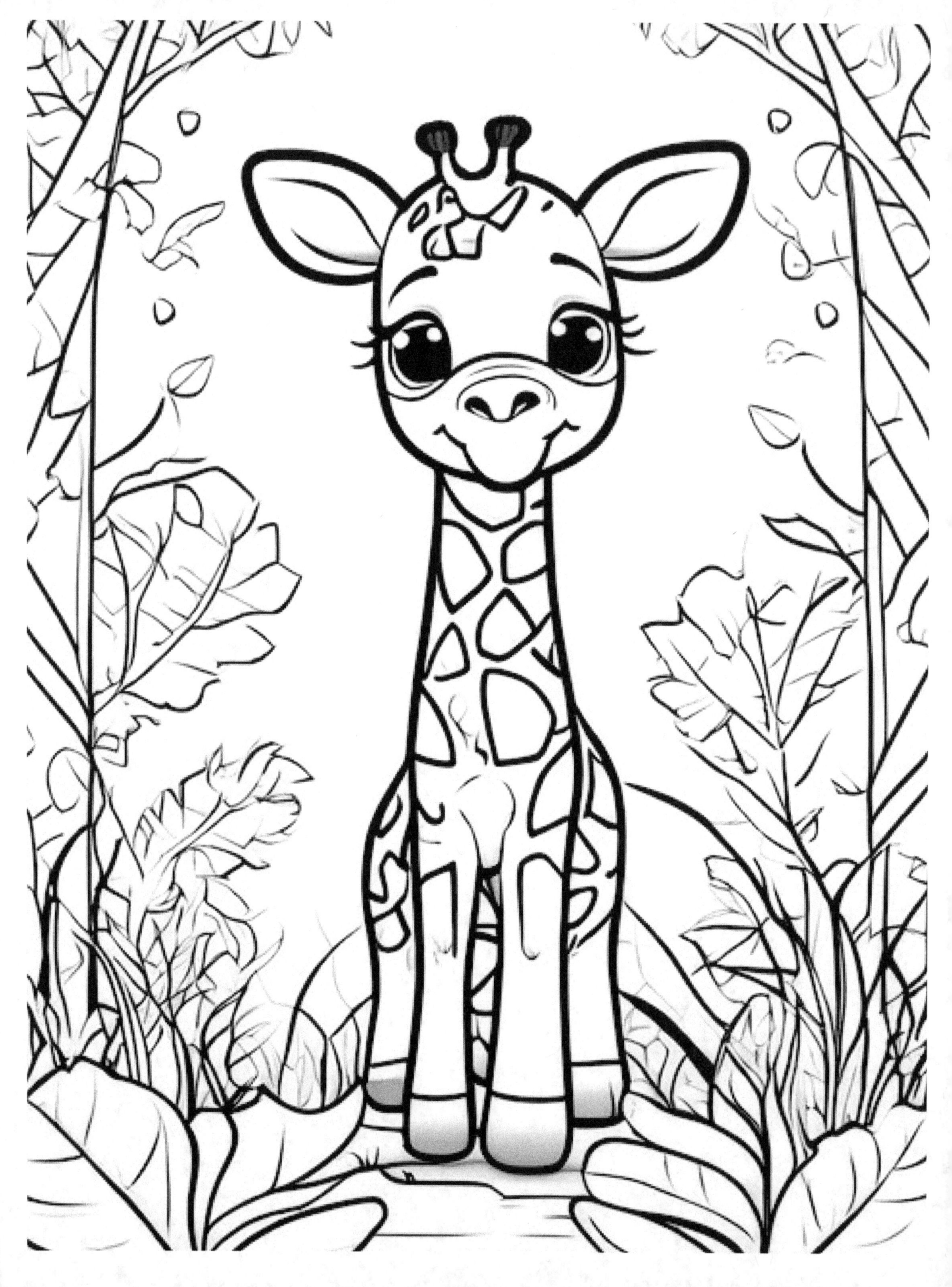

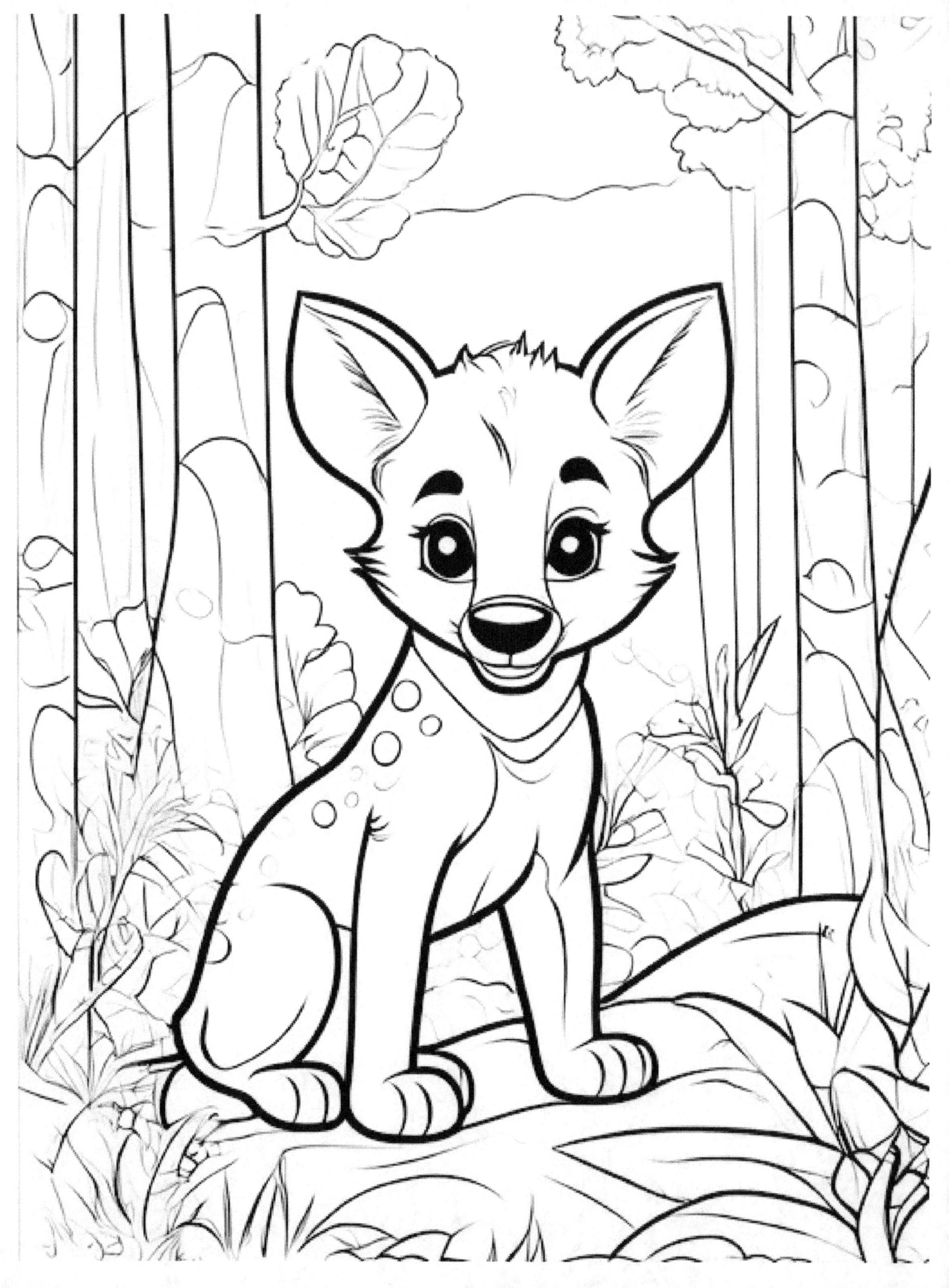

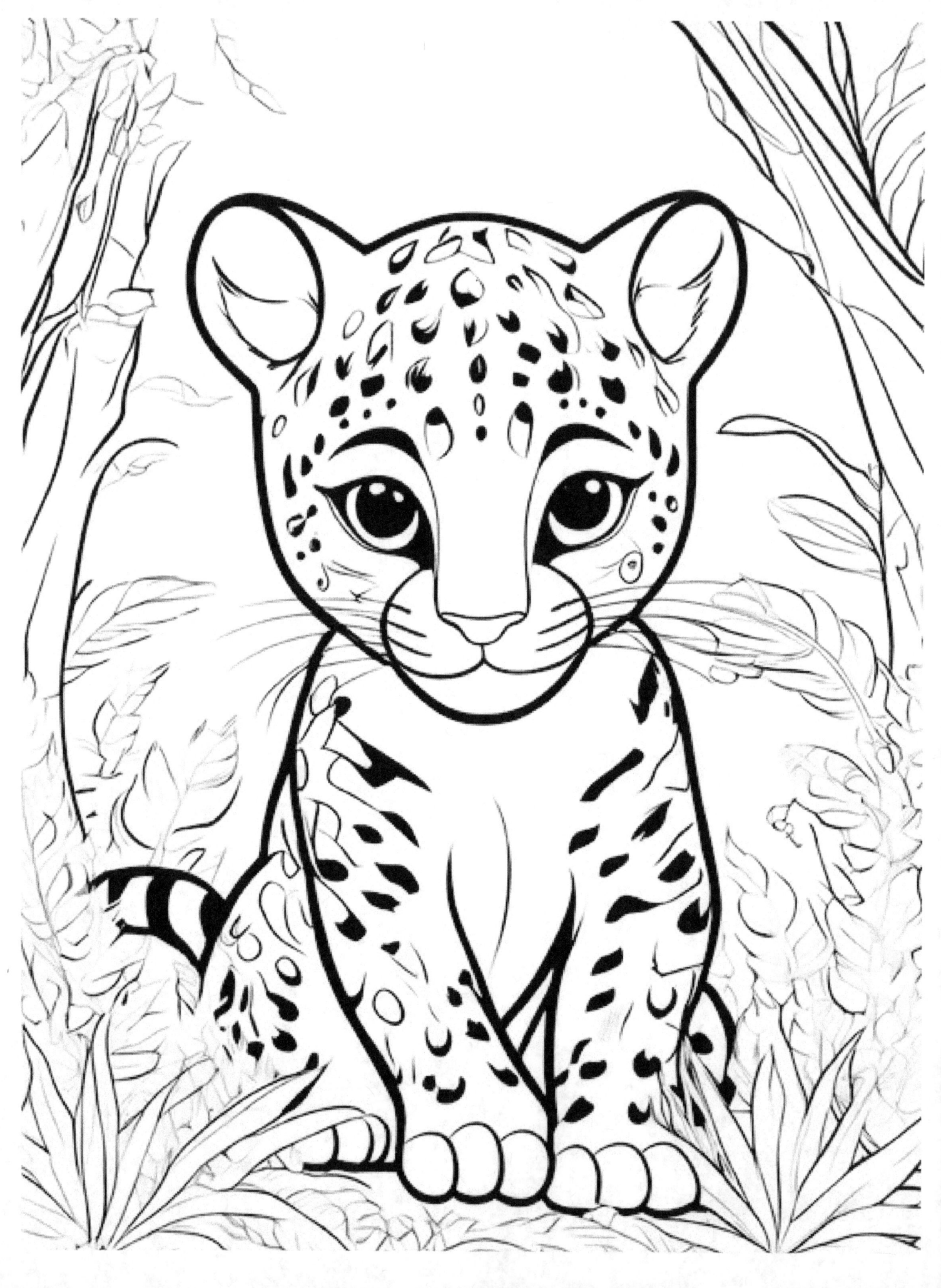

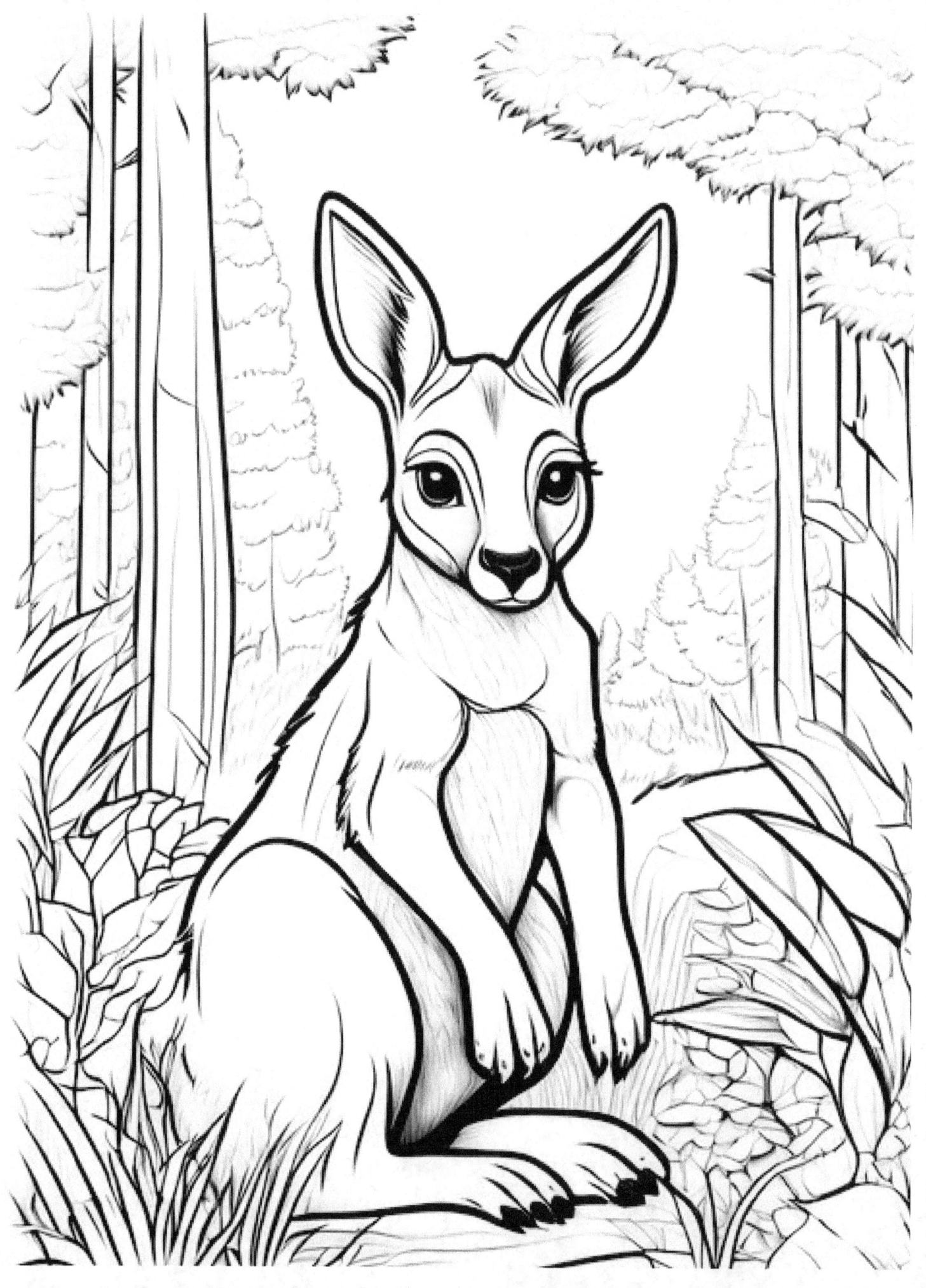

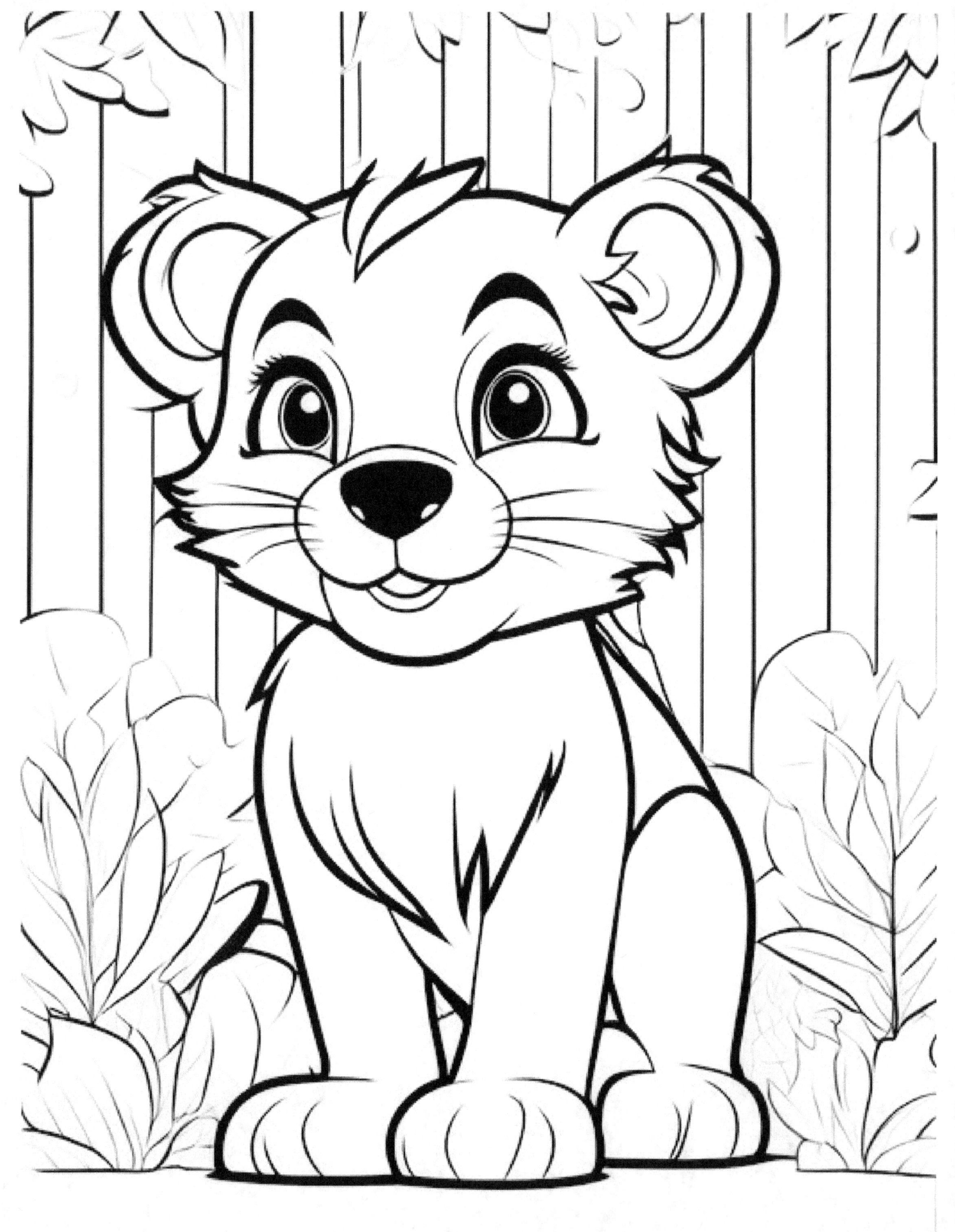

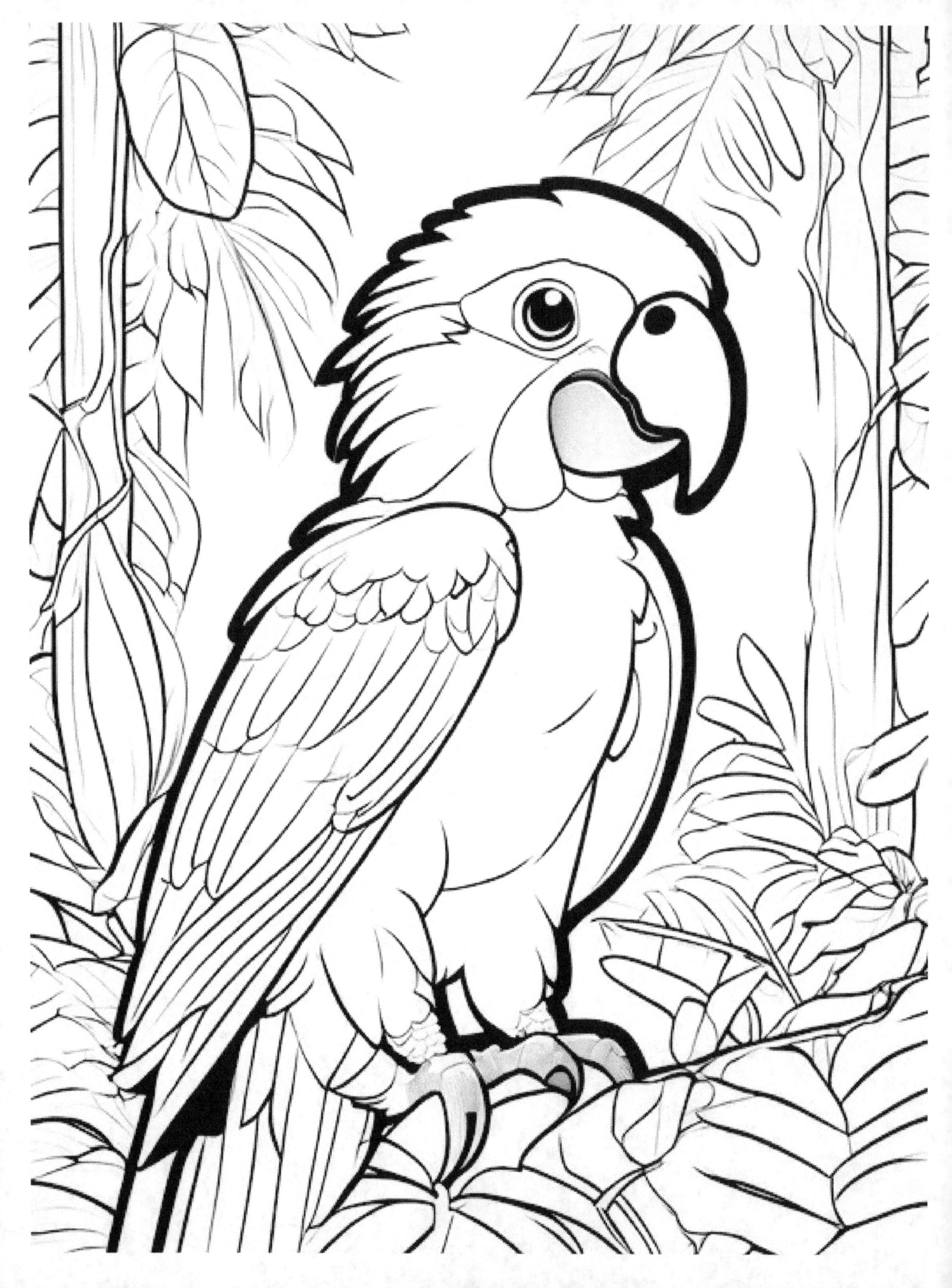

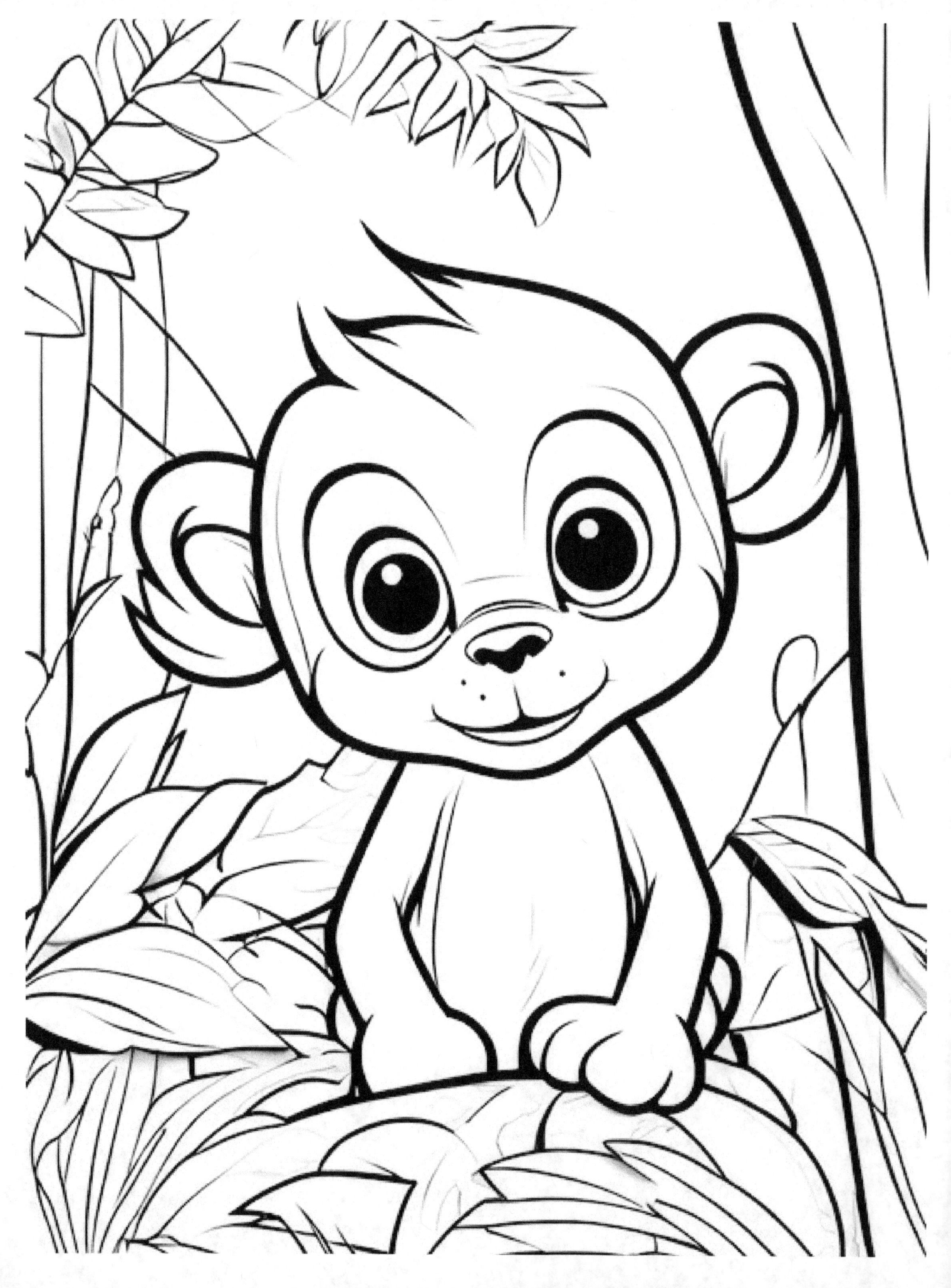

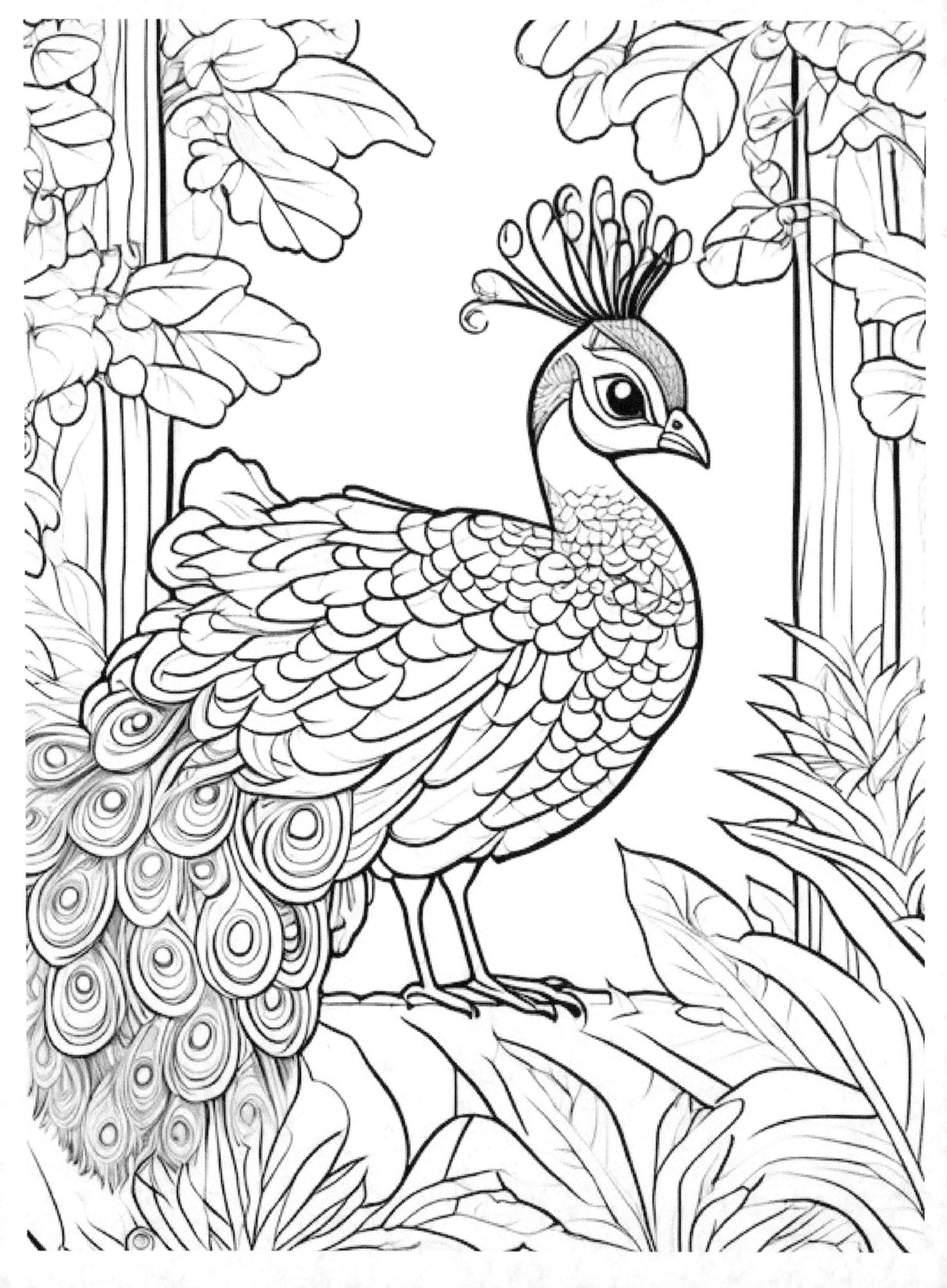

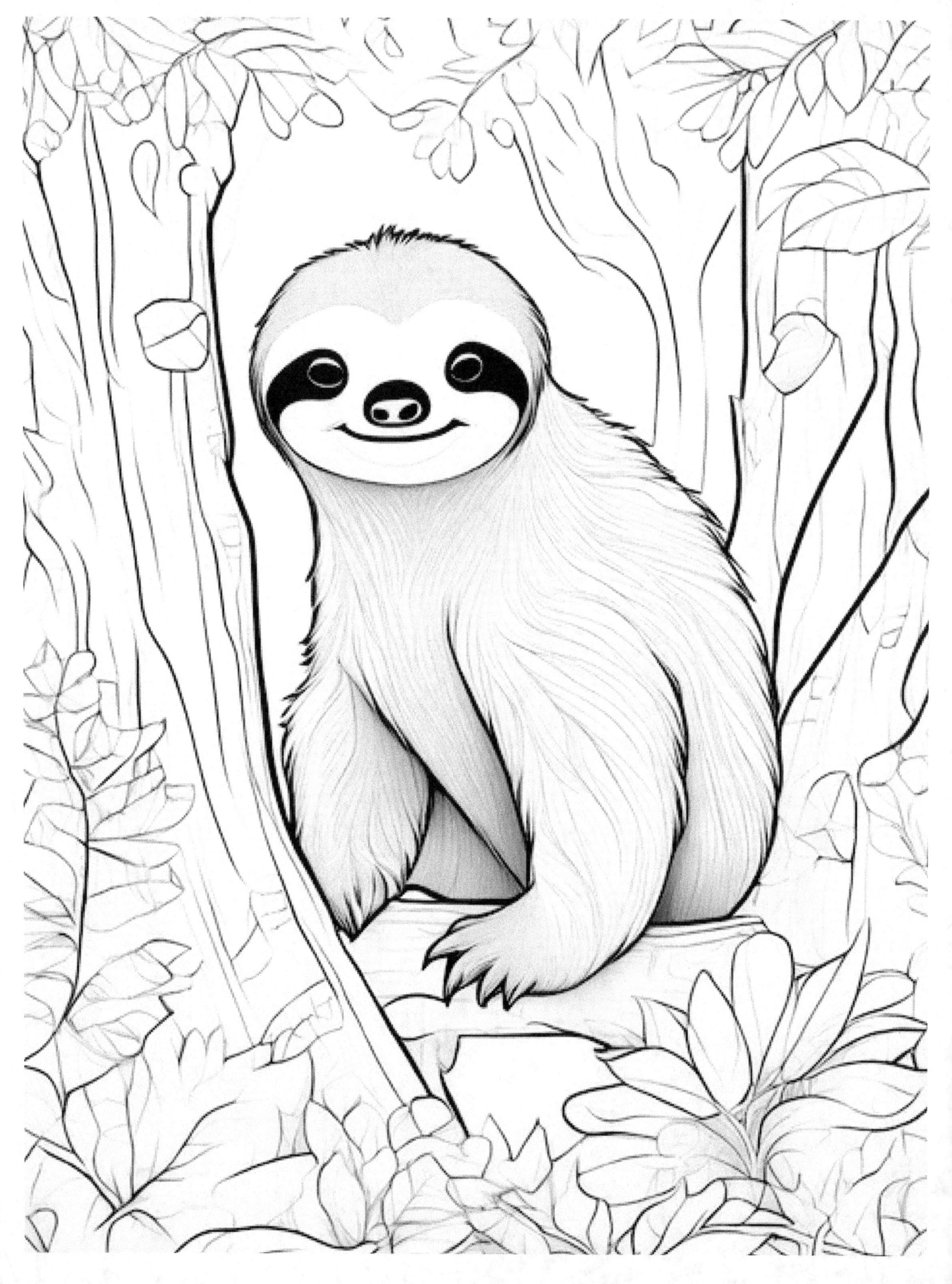

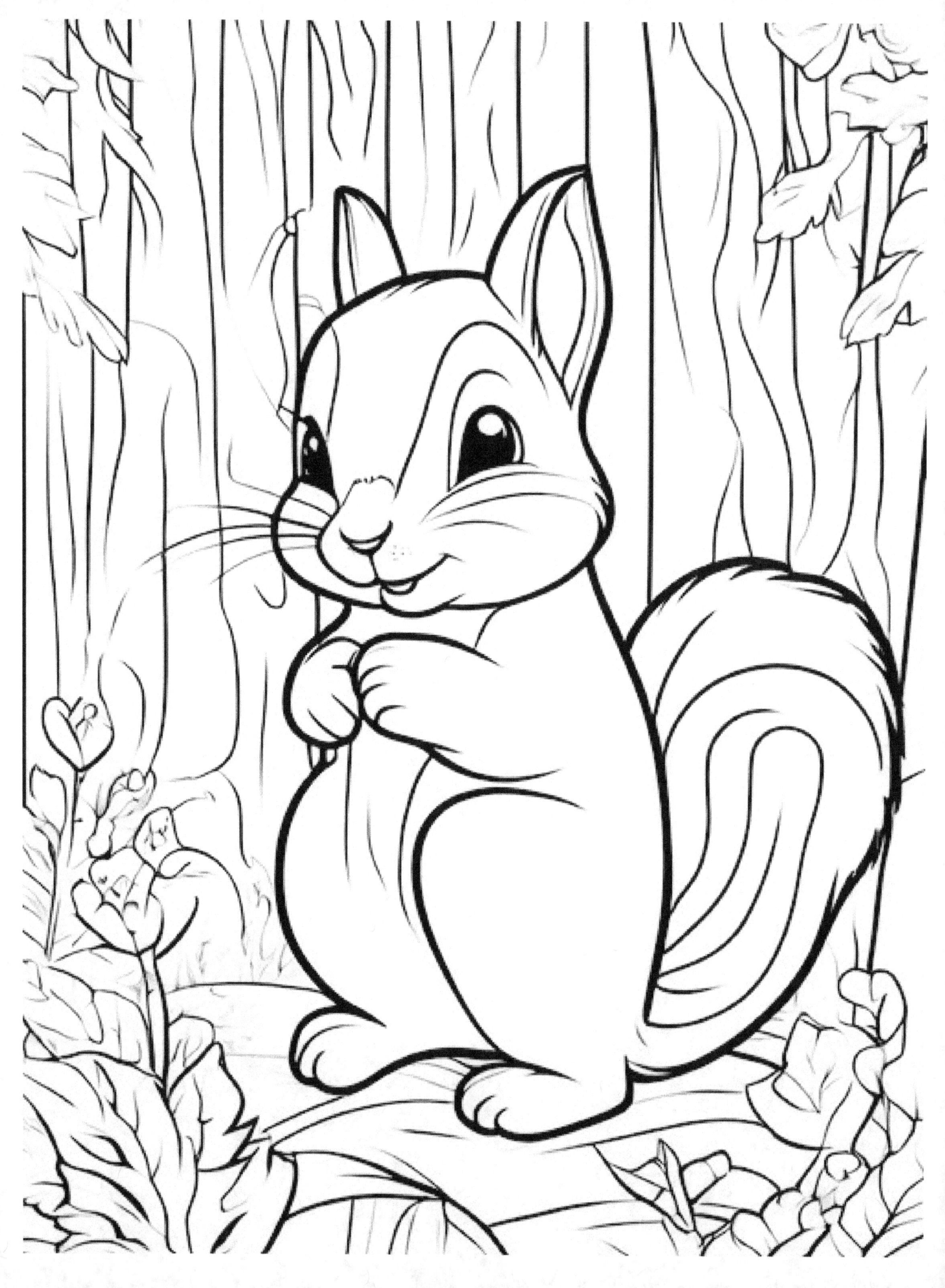

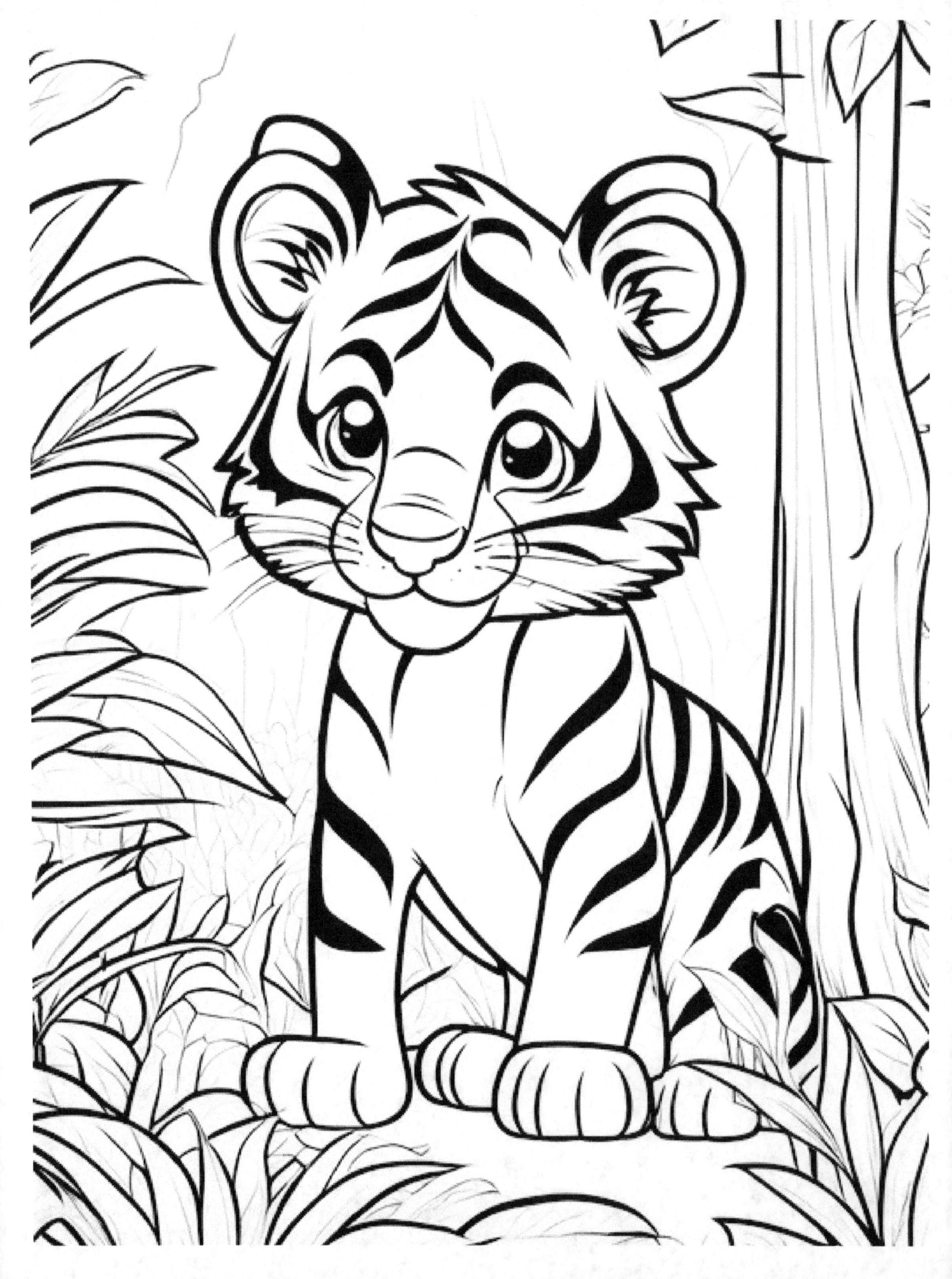

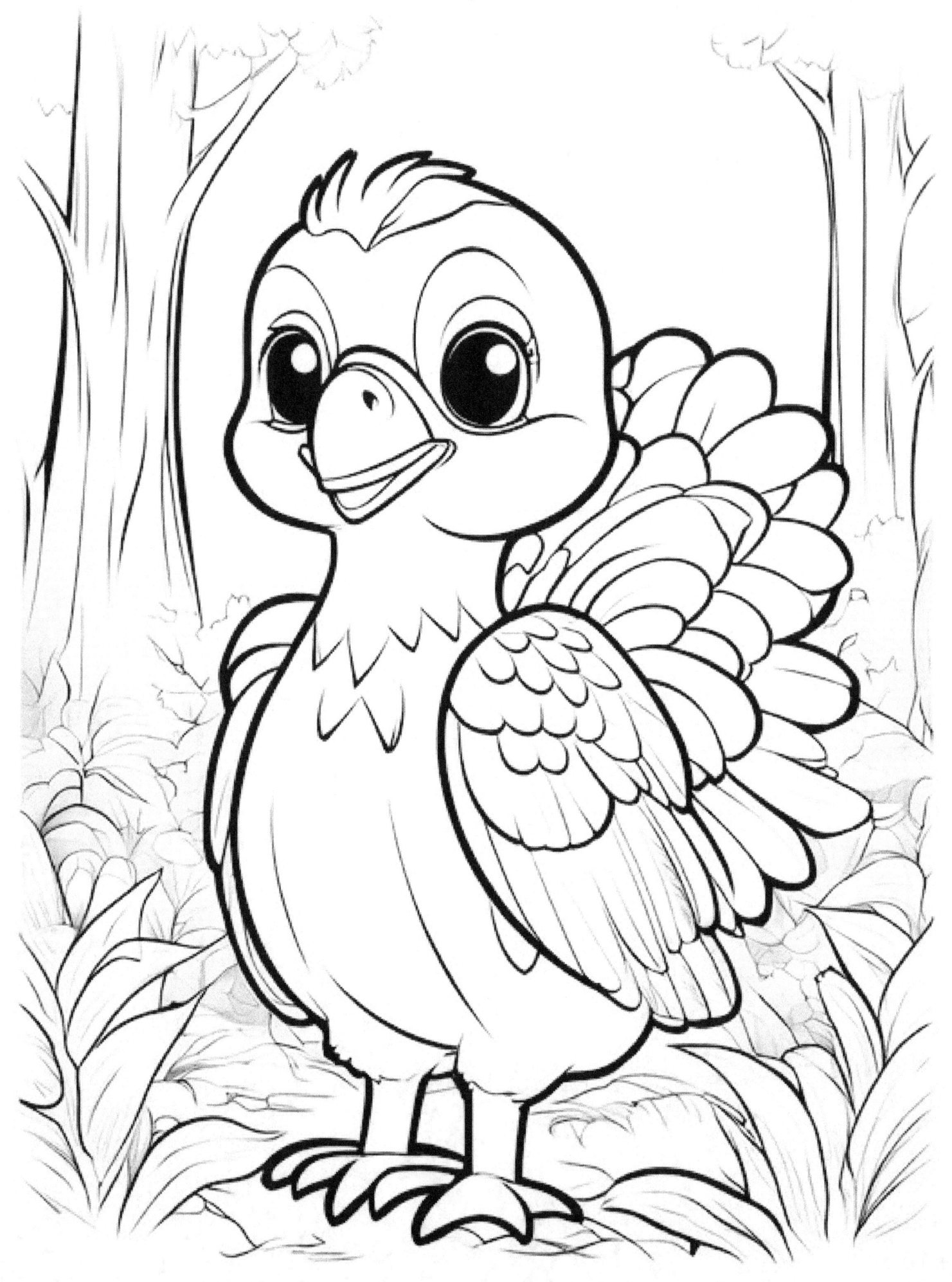

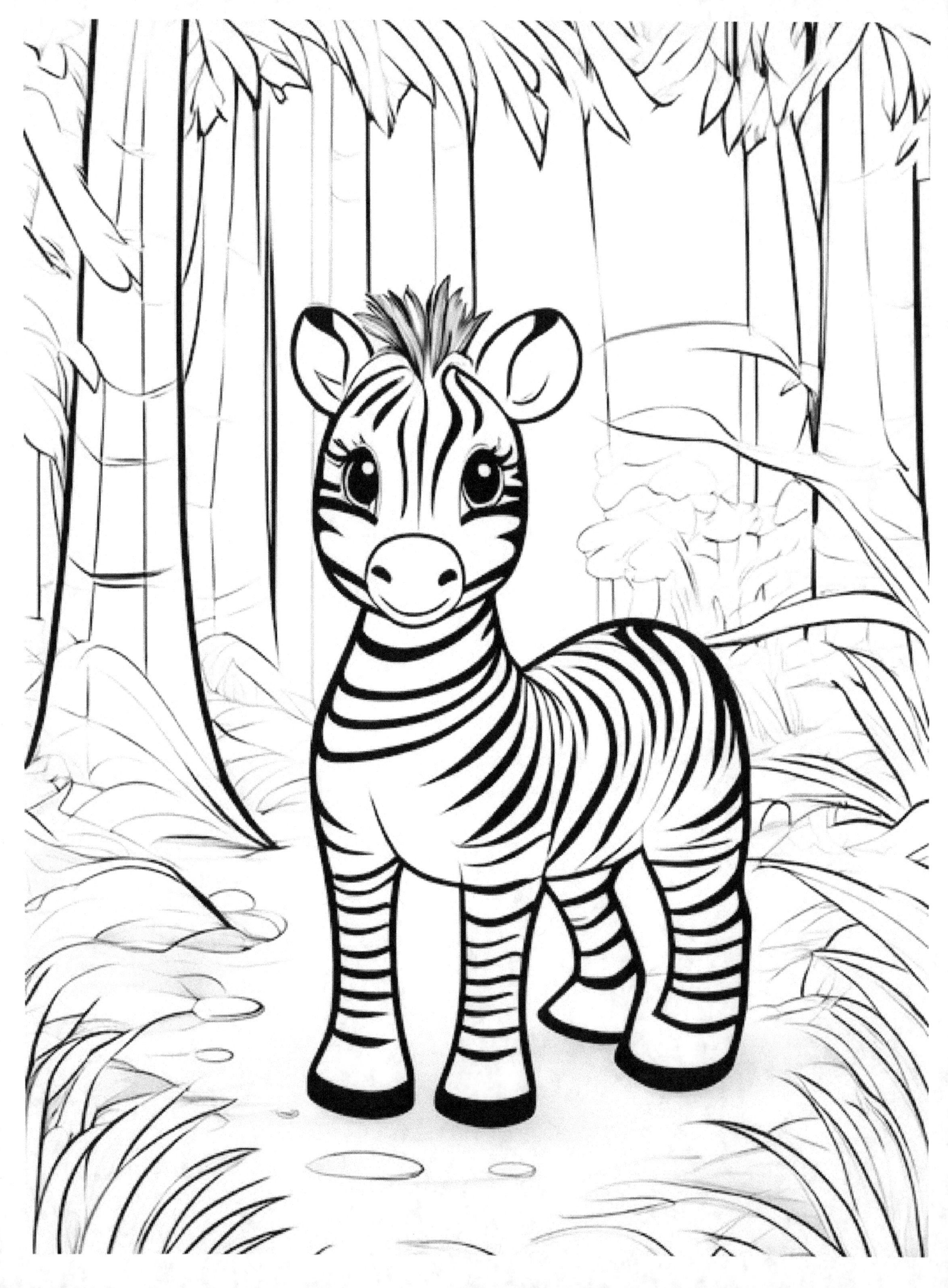